D0660247

ON TITAN

Chapter 1: The Titan's Son 1
Chapter 2: Her Determination 59
Chapter 3: Moonlit Oath 111
Trailer 165



87544965 8 Morgan 8/12/16

WAS THAT...
...A HUMAN HEAD?!
...!
HEATH...
H...
AAA
AATH!!

ゴォォォ

ゴーン
GONNNGG

ゴンポ
GONNNG

ZSH
OH...
OHHH...
OHHHH...
DSHUDD

CARLO PIKALE
AGE 18
SURVEY CORPS
SORUM HUMÉ
AGE 18
SURVEY CORPS
IS THIS...
GRRR
GRRR

GONNGG
ゴォォォ!

GONNGG
...HELL ?!

IT WAS THEM...
THE TITANS!
HAM
RATTLE
RATTLE
SORUM...
THAT'S RIGHT... EVEN THE SURVEY CORPS ISN'T IMMUNE TO THIS KIND OF FEAR...
HUFF!
RATTLE
HUFF!
RATTLE

BUT NOW...WE HUMANS HAVE FELT THAT FEAR...
IT ONLY TOOK 30 YEARS FOR US TO FORGET THE TERROR OF THE TITANS...
...CARVED DEEP INTO OUR HEARTS ONCE AGAIN...
MY WISH...

OUR WISH IS SIMPLE: TO OPEN THE GATES, AT ONCE. THAT IS ALL!

WHAT'S WITH THA LOT?
IT'S *THEM.* YOU KNOW...
OH, THE TITAN WORSHIP-ERS?
!!
WHAT ARE YOU DOING?! WHY ARE YOU **LEADING** THESE LUNATICS?!
I THOUGHT YOU WERE-
ELENA ?!

HAS SHE LOST HER SENSES...?
HEY...
THAT WOMAN AT THE FRONT... ISN'T SHE THE WIDOW OF SQUAD LEADER HEATH OF THE SURVEY CORPS?
SQUAD LEADER HEATH... WASN'T IT HIS HEAD THE TITANS THREW OVER THE WALL?
AND NOW HIS WIFE IS MIXED UP WITH THOSE FREAKS WHO WORSHIP THE TITANS? IT'S LIKE A BAD JOKE.
OPEN THE GATE !!!
AND DELIVER US TO THE TITANS !!

OPEN THE GATE!
OPEN THE GATE!
OPEN THE GATE!
OPEN THE GATE!
RAAHHH
FOR THE WIFE OF A SURVEY CORPS SQUAD LEADER TO WORSHIP THE TITANS...! YOU CAN'T BE SERIOUS!
ELENA, DON'T DO THIS! STOP!!
REMEMBER, PREYING ON OTHERS' WEAKNESSES IS THEIR STANDARD OPERATING PROCEDURE.
CARLO...
UGH...
SORUM.
OPEN THE GATE!

OPEN THE GATE!
OPEN THE GATE!
OPEN THE GATE!
I SUPPOSE IT SUITED THEIR PURPOSES TO RECRUIT SOMEONE RELATED TO THE SURVEY CORPS.
AND THAT LED TO THIS UPRISING...?
IF IT WASN'T FOR *THAT*...
THE LOCAL GARRISON SHOULD BE ABLE TO SUPPRESS A DEMONSTRATION LIKE THIS.
STOPPING THESE LUNATICS ISN'T OUR JOB.
DAMN IT...

AHH...
AH-
AAAH...
JUST LOOK AT HIS FLABBY BODY.
PROBABLY CAME HERE FOR SOME BUSINESS DINNER.
THE FOOL WANDERED RIGHT INTO THIS.
THAT IDIOT OFFICIA FROM TH ROYAL COURT!
S E AN NT AR ED HE E.

GONNGG
ゴーン
THE LIBERTY BELL!!!
ゴーン GONNGG
ゴーン GONNG!
...!!
TRUE FREEDOM !!
GIVE US TRUE FREEDOM !!

GONNGG
WHA ...?
THOKK

DMM
GRR
GGG
GG
THE GATE...
RRGGGG
...IS OPENING ?
GRRGG
GGRGG
NO...YOU CAN'T...
GGRRRG
THERE ARE PEOPLE HERE...

GONNGG
RRGGHH
GRRGGG
GONNNG
CLAANG
GONNNG
THE GATE'S OPENING.
GONNNGG
HEY, PAPA...
GONNNGG

THUD...
THUD...
THUD...
HEY...
GONNGG
GONNGG
THUD...
THUD...
THAT SOUND ...
FOOT-STEPS ...
THUD...
GONN
NNGG
IT'S A TITAN!
THUD...

THUD
ズーン!!
WHUP

GONNNG
GONNNG

GONNGG
GONNGG

ゴゴゴゴ！GONNNG ゴ

GRRT...
H-HEY, CARLO!
WHY DID THE TITAN GO BACK OUTSIDE THE WALL?
WHO CAN SAY?
ZSHH
I HEARD FROM THAT MOB WE JUST PASSED THAT SOME BRAVE CIVILIANS LURED IT OUT SO THE GATE COULD BE CLOSED AGAIN.
BUT PERHAPS... IT JUST WASN'T HUNGRY ANYMORE.
AT ANY RATE, WE'RE SOLDIERS. LET'S ACT LIKE IT.
WE NEED TO FIGURE OUT THE SITUATION AND REPORT TO THE HIGHER-UPS.

CLUNK
THE BODIES WILL HAVE TO BE MOVED QUICKLY...
TO PREVENT DISEASE, YOU MEAN?
WE CAN'T DENY THE POSSIBILITY THAT THE TITAN BROUGHT SICKNESS IN WITH IT, AS WELL.
BESIDES...

...THEY JUST SPIT THEIR VICTIMS OUT, HALF-DIGESTED.
THEY CAN'T REST IN PEACE LIKE THIS.

IF YOU CAN'T KEEP THEM DOWN, DON'T EAT THEM!
WHAK
...
BUT...IF WE DON'T AT LEAST TRY, WE'LL ALWAYS BE NOTHING MORE THAN THEIR PREY.
I DON'T THINK I WANT TO UNDER-STAND THEM.
THEIR ACTIONS MAKE NO SENSE!
IT'S SICKENING...
MAN...
WHAT A WAY TO EAT.

CLOTHES AND EQUIPMENT WHOLE...
NOT EVEN CLOSE TO FULLY DIGESTED.
SINCE THEY'RE VOMITING IT ALL OUT, THEY CAN'T REALLY HAVE A SENSE OF TASTE.
!
LOOK AT THAT!

...IT'S ELENA!
SO THE ONE RESPONSIBLE FOR THIS IS DEAD...
...
IT COULDN'T HAVE TURNED OUT ANY WORSE...
...SUCH A SHAME...
...WITH A BABY ON THE WAY...
NEWLY MARRIED

RUSTLE
HUH ...?
WHAT IS IT, CARLO ?
RUSTLE...
AT ANY RATE, WE CAN'T JUST LEAVE THEM HERE!
SORUM! GET IN TOUCH WITH THE GARRISON TROOPS AND ARRANGE A TEAM TO RETRIEVE THIS-
DSH

RUSTLE
RUSTLE
RUSTLE

NO WAY! IS SHE ALIVE-?
NO!
GRLK
GRLK
GRLK
HEY ...
YOU DON'T THINK ...

WE DON'T KNOW A THING ABOUT THEIR PHYSIOL-OGY!!
BUT ARE YOU CERTAIN ?!
NO WAY...
...IT'S POSSIBLE... THAT NEW TITANS ARE BORN FROM THE TITANS' VOMIT...?
GRRK
GRRK
GRRK
WHAT IF-?!
WHAT IF THERE IS THE SEED OF A NEW TITAN IN THAT VOMIT...?
WE CAN'T LET THAT HELL COME BACK HERE TO SHIGANSHINA DISTRICT AGAIN!!
DO IT...

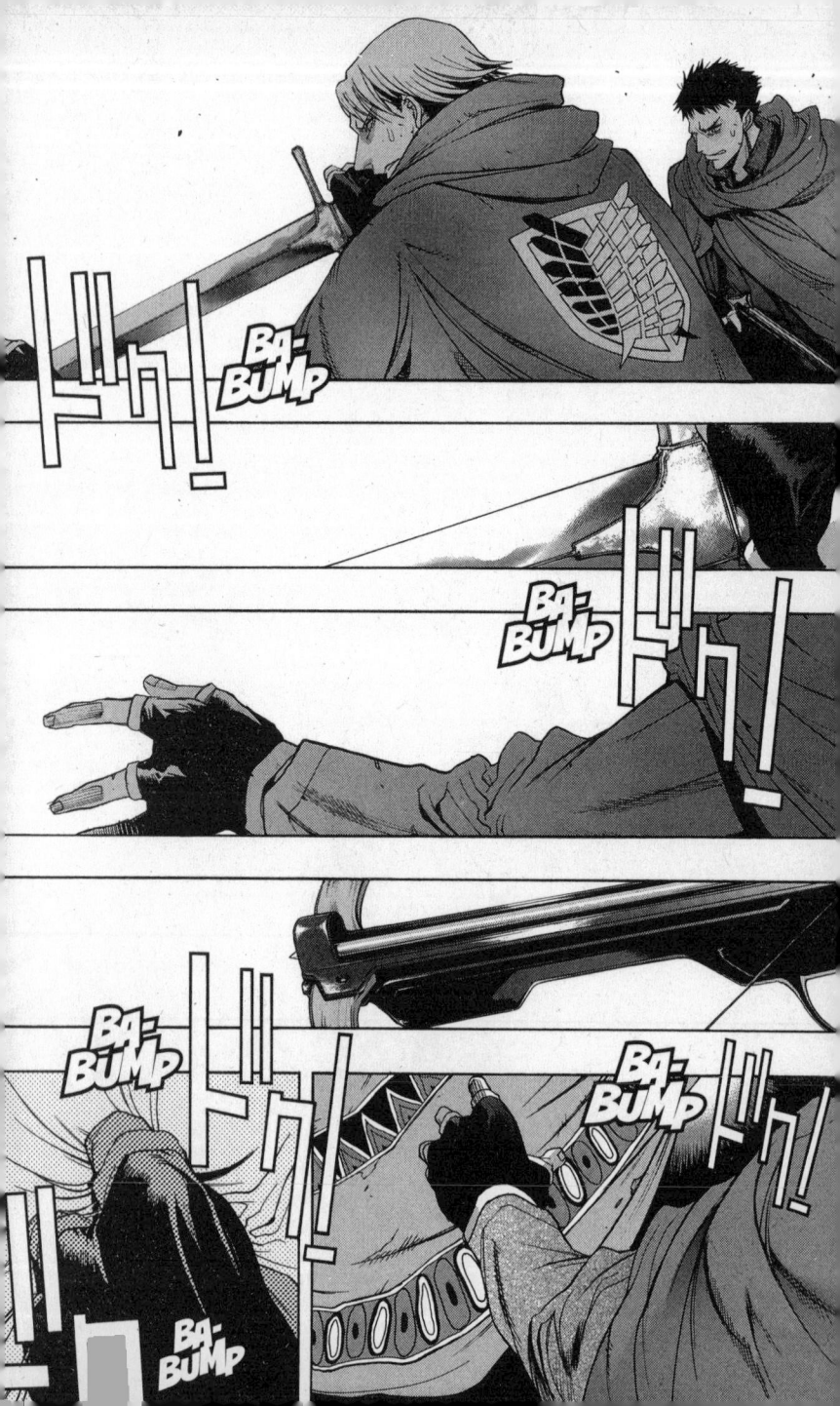
ドッ!
BA-BUMP
BA-BUMP
ドッ!
BA-BUMP
ドッ!
BA-BUMP
ドッ!
BA-BUMP

BA-BUMP
BA-BUMP
BA-BUMP
BA-BUMP
A...

A BABY ...?!
IT WAS ALIVE...
...STILL ALIVE INSIDE OF ELENA... AFTER THE TITAN ATE HER!!

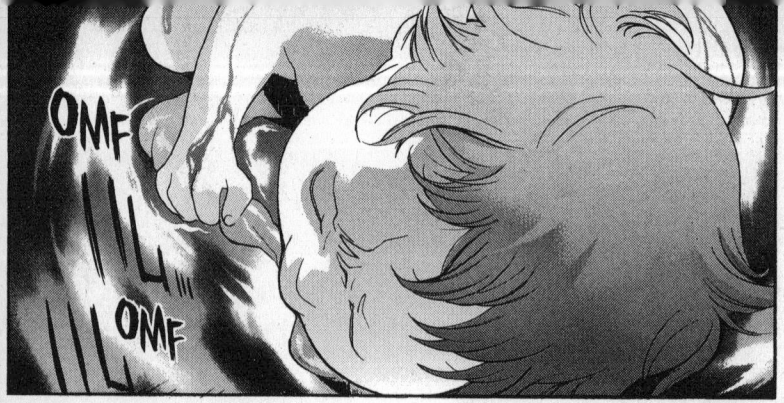
OMF
OMF

WHY ...?
WHY ONLY YOU ...?

...
IT'S...

THE SON... OF A TITAN...

Thirteen years later...

KRKK
GRAAH
AMAZIN

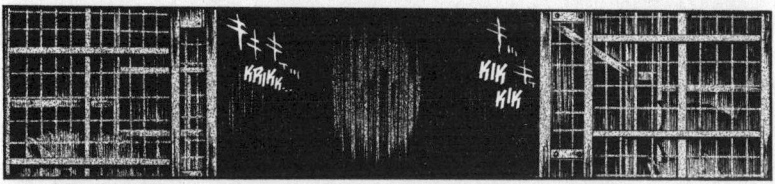
KRIKK...
KIK
KIK

Chapter 1: The Titan's Son END

ATTACK ON TITAN

BEFORE THE FALL

THE TITAN ASSAULT ON SHIGANSHINA DISTRICT.
THIS UNPRECEDENTED INCIDENT CAST HUMANITY FROM A THIRTY-YEAR PERIOD OF SECURITY INTO THE DEPTHS OF TERROR.
IN THE END, OVER FIVE THOUSAND WERE KILLED OR WENT MISSING, AND OVER A HUNDRED HOMES WERE DESTROYED—STAGGERING NUMBERS, ALL CAUSED BY A SINGLE TITAN.
THE PEOPLE OF SHIGANSHINA WERE STUNNED AND TERRIFIED BY THE TITAN'S WRATH, AND LOST ALL TRUST IN THE MILITARY AND THE ROYAL GOVERNMENT FOR THEIR ROLE IN THE DISASTER.

THIRTEEN YEARS LATER...
Chapter 2: Her Determination

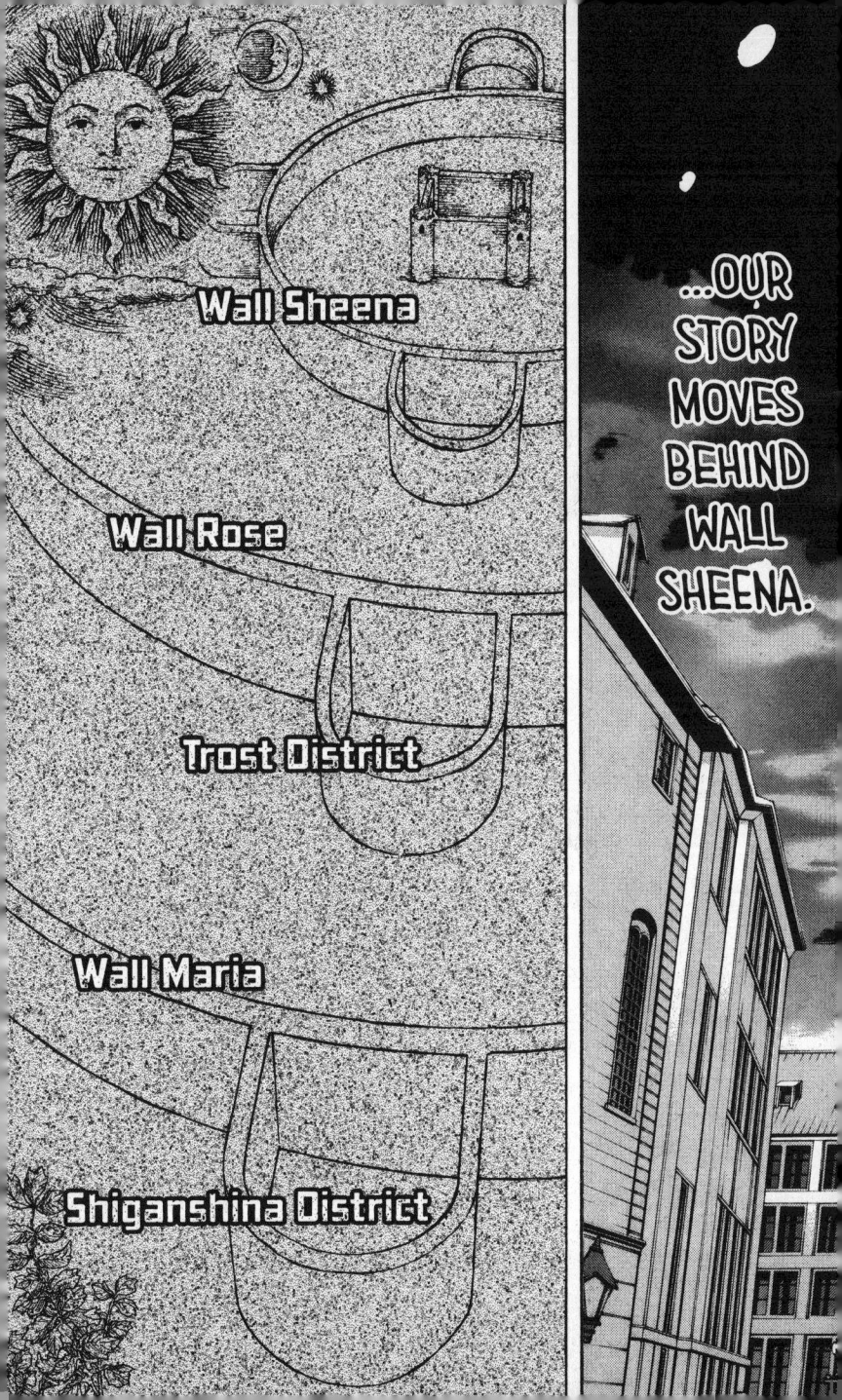
Wall Sheena
Wall Rose
Trost District
Wall Maria
Shiganshina District
...OUR STORY MOVES BEHIND WALL SHEENA.

TOKK
TOKK
THUD
TOKK
THUD
TOKK
TOKK
SO THIS IS THE ONE...

...
!!
DON'T BE CONCERNED, SIR. HE WON'T BITE.
LOOM
DO
DT BE
OLED.
HE LOOKS LIKE ANY OTHER BOY TO ME.
IS THAT REALLY HIM IN THERE?
HEE HEE ...
YOU'RE IN CHARGE HERE?

WHAT MAN WOULD LIE TO THE FACE OF THE GREAT MERCHANT DARIO INOCENCIO...
...ONE OF THE RICHEST MEN IN THE INTERIOR!
THIS IS THE VERY BOY...
THE CHILD BORN OF THE TITAN'S FILTH...
NOW, GAZE UPON THE FACE...

...OF THE TITAN'S SON...
...KUKLO!!!
KH...

HERE!
BAH!
ZM
MF
SO HAVE YOU, OLD MAN.
HEE HEE! YOU'VE MADE AN EXCELLENT DEAL.
MANY THANKS, MY LORD...
WHO WAS THIS ECCEN-TRIC?
OOPS! PARDON MY LANGUAGE, HEE HEE...
ECCEN-TRIC?
THERE WA ANOTHER ECCENTR WHO EXPRESSE AN INTERE IN KUKLO WELL.

HO CAN
AY? NOT
ME, FOR
ERTAIN...
WHAT DID HE WANT WITH THE TITAN'S SON?
A MOST GLOOMY MAN, DRESSED IN BLACK RAGS...
BUT HE HAD TO HAVE THE BOY, OR SO HE CLAIMED...
OPPOR-TUNIST KNAVE.
EE
EE!
REASONS ASIDE, I ALWAYS PLANNED TO GIVE YOU THE BOY, MASTER.
NOR DO I.
I DON'T UNDERSTAND.

IT STINKS.
INDEED, IT STINKS HERE.
THANK YOU.
NOW THAT OUR BUSINESS IS FINISHED, LET'S BE AWAY FROM THIS FETID PLACE.
WELL, I'LL SEE TO IT THAT HE' TRANSPORTE TO YOUR MANSION.

ガラ
RATTLE
ガラ
RATTLE

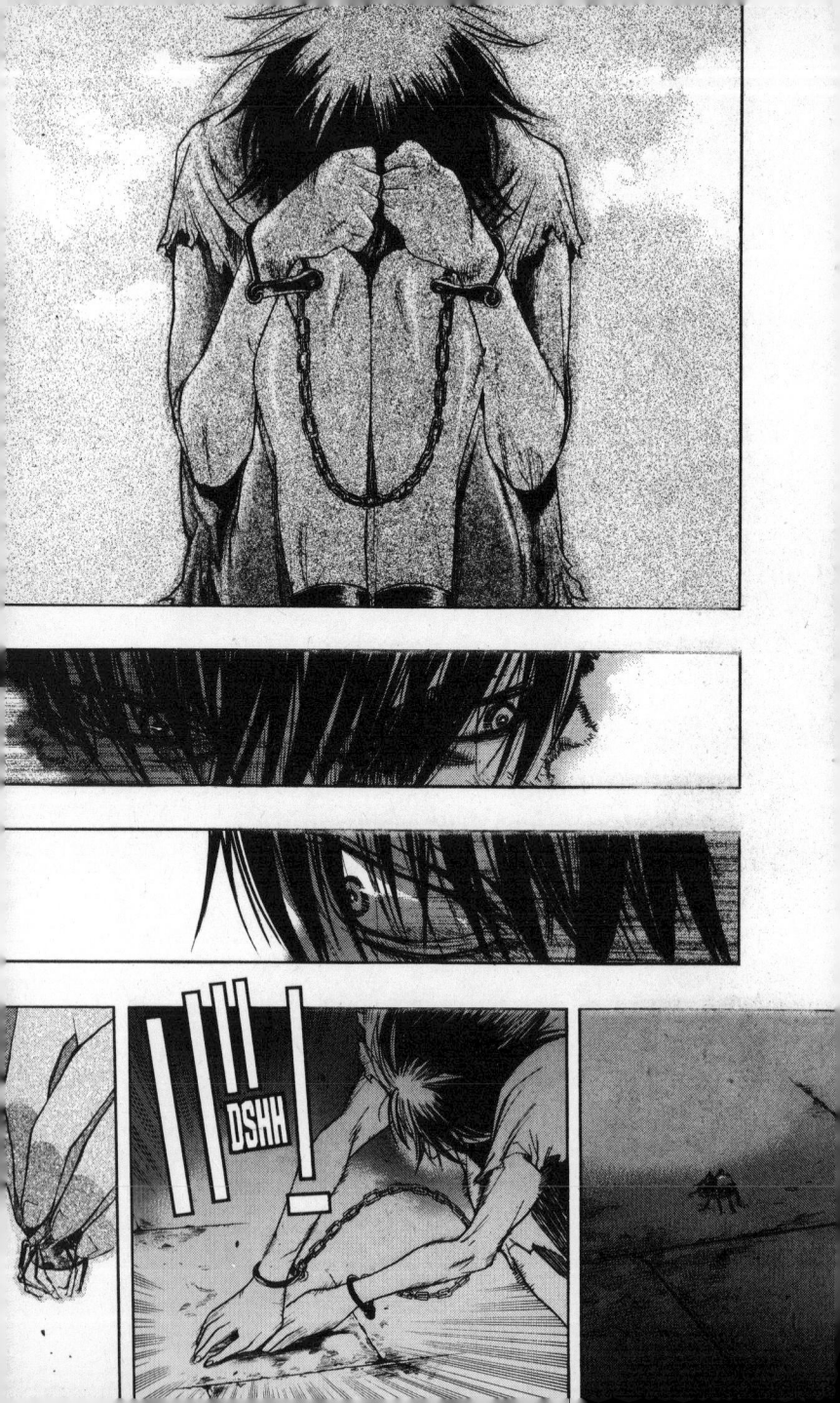
DSHH

KRCH...
クチ..
GRSH
グチュ.
グチ
GRSH
STOMP
WHAM
STOMP
STOMP
STOMP
STOMP

?!!
AHA HA!
THERE HE IS!
SO THIS IS KUKLO !
IS HE A TITAN?

DON'T GET TOO CLOSE. BE CAREFUL...
HE'S STILL JUST A KID!
...XAVI.
HE'S CHAINED UP, ANYWAY.
I'M FINE.

THUD
I KNOW, I KNOW!
THUD
THINK OF THIS AS AN INVESTMENT TOWARD THAT GOAL-
YOU'RE GOING TO BE HEAD OF THE MILITARY SOMEDAY, XAVI.
THUD
KA
THWAK
HUH?
SEE? I'LL DESTROY ALL THE TITANS MYSELF!

HE'S SUCH A WEAKLING !!

SPLASH
?!
BWAH
GAHK!
HAHK!

GLUNK
GAHAK!
KFF KOFF!
SHIVER
GAHH!
FOR A TITAN, YOU SURE SLEEP A LOT.
KA-HAK...
SHH
HUFF...
SPLATCH
HEF!
HEF!
HUFF!
HUFF!
YOU SHOULD BE GRATEFUL THAT I COME DOWN HERE TO WAKE YOU UP EVERY MORNING.

TCH!
YOU'RE SO WEAK, YOU'RE NOT EVEN WORTH BEATING.
SLURP
THWUD
WELL ?!
HUH ?!
SPEAK UP, TITAN !!
URGH !
FIGHT BACK A LITTLE, WHY DON'T YOU?
THIS IS NO FUN.
FIGHT BACK. FIGHT. BACK.
... GHT ...
CK
FI...
...T BA...
... BA... CK...

URGH...
フラ
YES, THAT'S MUCH...
FI... GHT ...
... BACK ...
... BA ...
IGH

WHUK
...BETTER !!
SWOOP
BSHT
SEE, YOU CAN DO IT AFTER ALL!!
FWUMP
GAHK...

BLEGH!
ULP...
BLEGH!
KTHUD
GRFH !!
YOU TITANS...
...EAT PEOPLE, DON'T YOU?
I SAW ONE IN SHIGANSHINA ABOUT A MONTH AGO.
I DIDN'T GET TO SEE IT EAT ANYONE, OF COURSE...
WHUMP
WHUMP
WHACK

WHUMP
SO WHAT DO HUMANS TASTE LIKE, ANYWAY?!
I BET WE'RE ELICIOUS !
WHUMP
TWITCH
TWITCH!
HUFF...
FF...
ROLL...
DO YOU GAIN A TITAN'S STRENGTH IF YOU EAT IT?!
I WONDER IF YOU CAN EAT TITANS, TOO...?

CHOMP
HRRG.
AAH...
BWAH!
BLEGH!
AHH...
...HUH?

FIGHT ...
... BACK ...
DID I GO A LITTLE TOO FAR?
OH, WELL.
YOU'RE A TITAN. YOU CAN'T BREAK DOWN SO EASILY.
THAT'S RIGHT.
FIGHT ...
BACK ...
SHOMP
EAT IT ALL, NOW.

KSH
KCHAK
CHONP
CHONP
KSH...
KRK

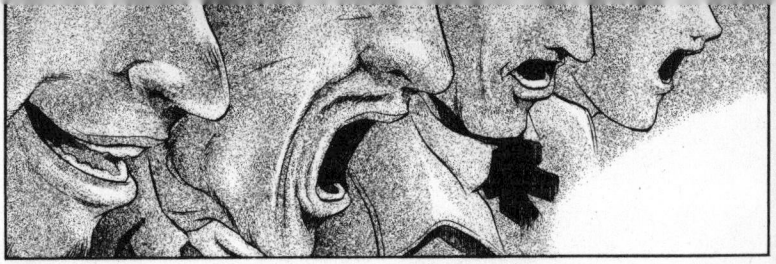

TITAN'S... SON...

WH O OOO SH
RATTLE
RATTLE

SQUEEZE
...I'M SCARED...

THERE'S A TITAN IN OUR HOUSE...

I GUESS FATHER MUST KNOW WHAT HE'S DOING, FOR BROTHER'S SAKE...

BUT... I JUST DON'T THINK...

...IT SHOULD BE LIVING IN OUR HOUSE...

THAT TITAN...
THAT MONSTER...
I'VE GOT TO...

WOO-HOOO!!
FINALLY, WALL MARIA! THE FARTHEST REACHES OF OUR TERRITORY!!
SO THE TITANS ARE REALLY JUST ON THE OTHER SIDE OF THIS WALL?!!

IT WAS WORTH COMING TO SHIGANSHINA FOR OUR FAMILY VACATION, FATHER!
I'D NEVER SEE WALL MARIA IF I SPENT MY WHOLE LIFE TRAPPED BEHIND WALL SHEENA!
RIGHT, FATHER ?!
!
TSK!
HAVEN'T THEY FINISHED TALKING YET?
THEY WON'T LET US THROUGH THAT EASILY...
AFTER ALL, WHO DECIDES TO VISIT THE WALL MARIA RESTRICTED AREA ON A WHIM?
OF COURSE...

I AM CURIOUS...
...ABOUT THE OUTSIDE WORLD...
JUST NOT LIKE THIS...

THAT'S RIGHT!
REALLY ?!
IT'S ALL SETTLED. WE'RE FREE TO GO.
WE'RE GOING ATOP THE WALL!
I'LL BE FIRST TO THE TOP!!
YAHOO!

ZSH...
I WONDER WHAT THE OUTSIDE WORLD...
...LOOKS LIKE...

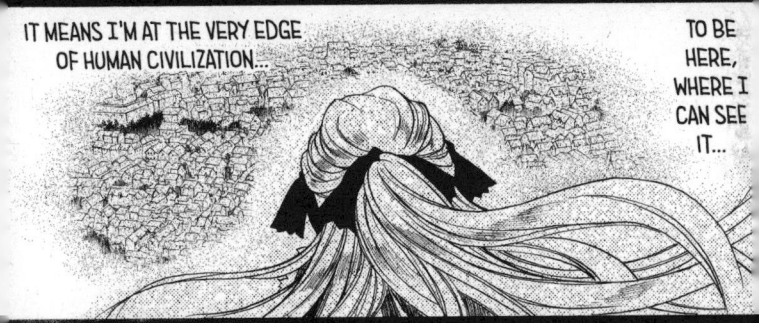

ND BEYOND
IS WALL IS...

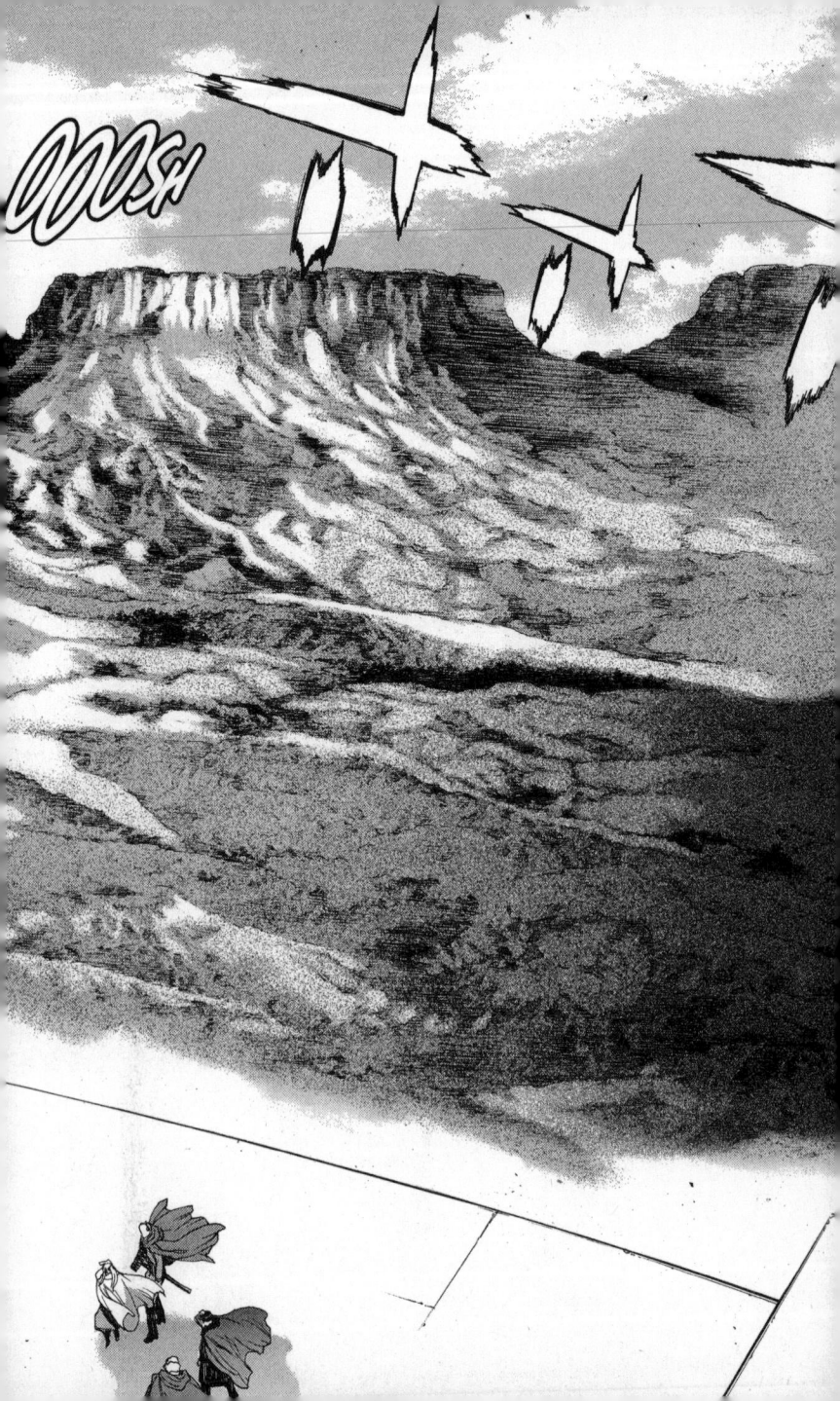
GOOSH

ESTOOOO

OHOH
WHO
OHOSH
SO THIS...
...IS THE OUTSIDE... WORLD...
THE ONLY REASON WE CAN'T KNOW THE ANSWER... IS...
WHAT'S BEYOND WHAT I CAN SEE?
WHAT IF THERE'S A STRANGE LAND OVER THE HORIZON, AND IT JUST WASN'T IN THE OLD BOOKS?
THERE'S NOTHING OUT THERE... JUST AN EMPTY... WASTE-LAND...

A TITAN !!!
COME AND SEE, FATHER!
WHOOSH
LOOK! IT'S OVER THERE!
YOU'VE FOUND ONE ALREADY, XAVI? THAT'S MY BOY!
HA-HA!
AH...
AH...
AAAH!

SHARLE?!
HOW CAN THEY DO IT...?
HOW CAN THEY LET SUCH A MONSTER INTO OUR HOME...?

I CAN'T LET IT LIVE...
...TO KILL THE TITAN'S SON!
I HAVE TO BE THE ONE...

Chapter 7: Her Determination END

ATTACK ON TITAN

BEFORE THE FALL

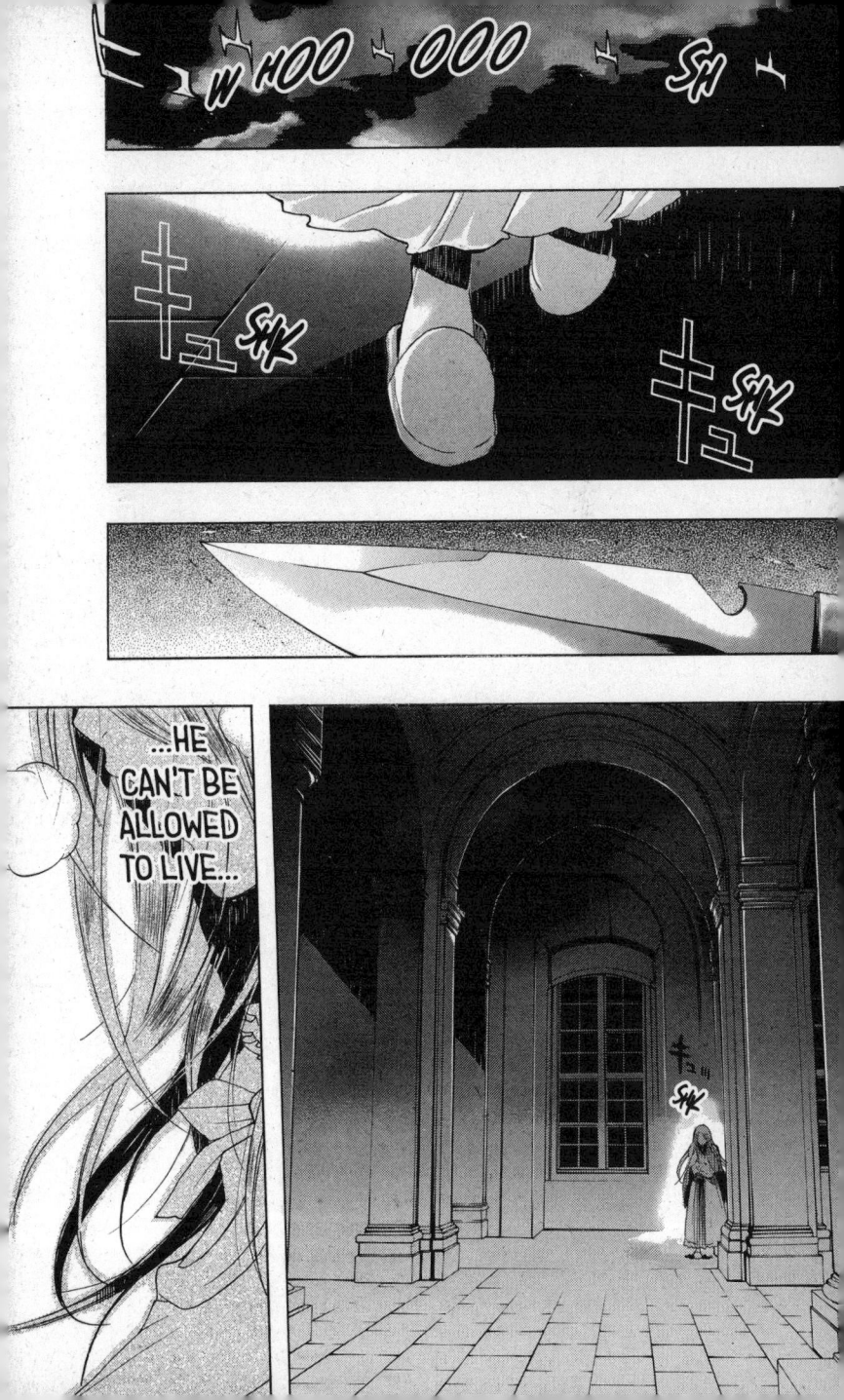
WHOO OOO
SH
SHK
SHK
SHK
...HE CAN'T BE ALLOWED TO LIVE...

# Chapter 3: Moonlit Oath

IF NO ONE ELSE IS GOING TO DO IT...
I HAVE TO KILL THE TITAN'S SON!

MY FATHER HAS SEEN ME AS NOTHING BUT A PAWN, TO BE MARRIED OFF TO SERVE SOME NEED.
FROM THE MOMENT I WAS BORN INTO THE INOCENCIO FAMILY...
...EVEN IF I DIE DOING IT...
BUT IF I CAN SAVE THE PEOPLE OF THIS TOWN BY KILLING THE TITAN'S SON...
...AT LEAST MY LIFE WILL HAVE MEANING.

CHK
CHK
CHK
CLICK
カチャ
!

ギィィィ
CREAAAK

CHATTER
CHATTER
WAVER...
FIGHT... BACK...
THIS...
...IS A TITAN...?

P-PLEASE...
DON'T FIGHT BACK...
FLINCH
LURCH
CLANK
CLANK
AH...
CLANK

H...
AAAH ...!
GRAB
AAH!
YANK
EEK!
SNAG

HUH...?
WH...
WHAT DOES THIS MEAN ...?
?!
HRRG

CLANK
WAIT... WAIT!!
DO... DO YOU WANT TO DIE?!
SWISH
WHY WOULD YOU...?
WH-WHY WOULD YOU DO THAT?!
FIGHT BACK.
I CAME HERE TO KILL YOU, AND YET...
HEH... YOU COULD ASK ME THE SAME.

OF COURSE, YOU WOULD FIGHT BACK...
FIGHT BACK.
FIGHT BACK.
...HUH?
YOU CAN TALK?!
BUT YOU'RE A TITAN !!
XAVI.
THAT'S
...MY BROTH-ER...
XAVI.
XAVI.
XAVI IS MY BROTHER'S NAME...
A-ARE YOU...?

ARE YOU REALLY A TITAN'S SON?!
!!
GRRLK
GRGGG
D-DOES IT HURT? OR ARE YOU JUST HUNGRY ?!
GUURG
IS THAT SOUND COMING FROM YOUR STOMACH ?!
GRLLG

FIGHT... BACK...
FI...
GRRK
カラ
CLANK

RRK
GRRRK
GRRG

...
ACK
...
-FIGHT
...
GLURRG

キュ KK
KK キュ
KK
キュ

キュ GRRK...

YOU'RE JUST HUNGRY... RIGHT?!
ギュ
ILILILIL
GURRG
DROOL
だらり
F-FIGHT...
JANGLE
JANGLE
...BACK...
ダラ
...
ドン
SKEF
FIGHT...
...BA...

GRAB
CHOMP
CHOMP
SWISH
GASHK
SHUKK
...YOU'RE ...
YOU'RE... NOT A TITAN, ARE YOU...?
CHOMP

CHOMP CHOMP
THE TITANS I'VE SEEN ARE MONSTERS ...
...BUT YOU JUST LOOK LIKE A PERSON TO ME...
PLUS... I'VE NEVER READ ABOUT CHILD TITANS IN ANY BOOKS.
I GUESS IF YOU'RE NOT A TITAN, YOU WOULDN'T KNOW...
IS IT TRUE THAT IF A TITAN GETS HURT, IT JUST GETS BETTER ...
... RIGHT AWAY ?!

DID FATHER... BRING YOU HERE...?
LLP
LLP
LLP
GLP
GLP
CHOMP
GLUKK
PFWAHH

...NAME ...?
WHAT'S...
...YOUR NAME...?
YOU'RE NOT A TITAN, ARE YOU?

KUKLO.

I'M SHARLE.

KUKLO.
IT'S NICE TO MEET YOU...
...?

SHARLE...
NICE... MEET YOU...?

SO YOU WERE NEVER...
...A TITAN'S SON IN THE FIRST PLACE!
CHOMP CHOMP
JUST LIKE...
...SHARLE...
YOU'RE HUMAN! JUST LIKE ME!

WHAT IS... TITAN ...?
SHARLE ...
HMM?
YOU KNOW YOU SPEAK HAS GOTT BETT
I DON'T KNOW...
...
IT'S NOT IN ANY OF THE BOOKS...
NO ONE KNOWS WHAT THE TITANS REALLY ARE.
IT'S A MAP.
THIS IS...?

IT'S A DRAWING THAT REPRESENTS THE WORLD WE LIVE IN... I THINK.

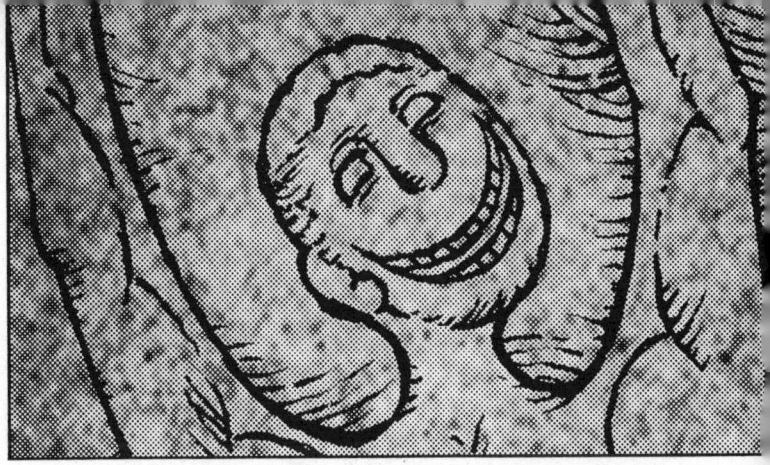

THE CIRCLE IN THE MIDDLE IS **WALL ROSE.**

AND THE ONE ON THE OUTSIDE IS **WALL MARIA.**

THIS CIRCLE IS A BIG WALL, CALLED **WALL SHEENA.**

THIS IS WHERE WE ARE NOW.

BUT HERE...
...
THIS IS THE ONLY PLACE HUMANS CAN LIVE.
...A MAN...
...TITAN...
THAT'S A TITAN.

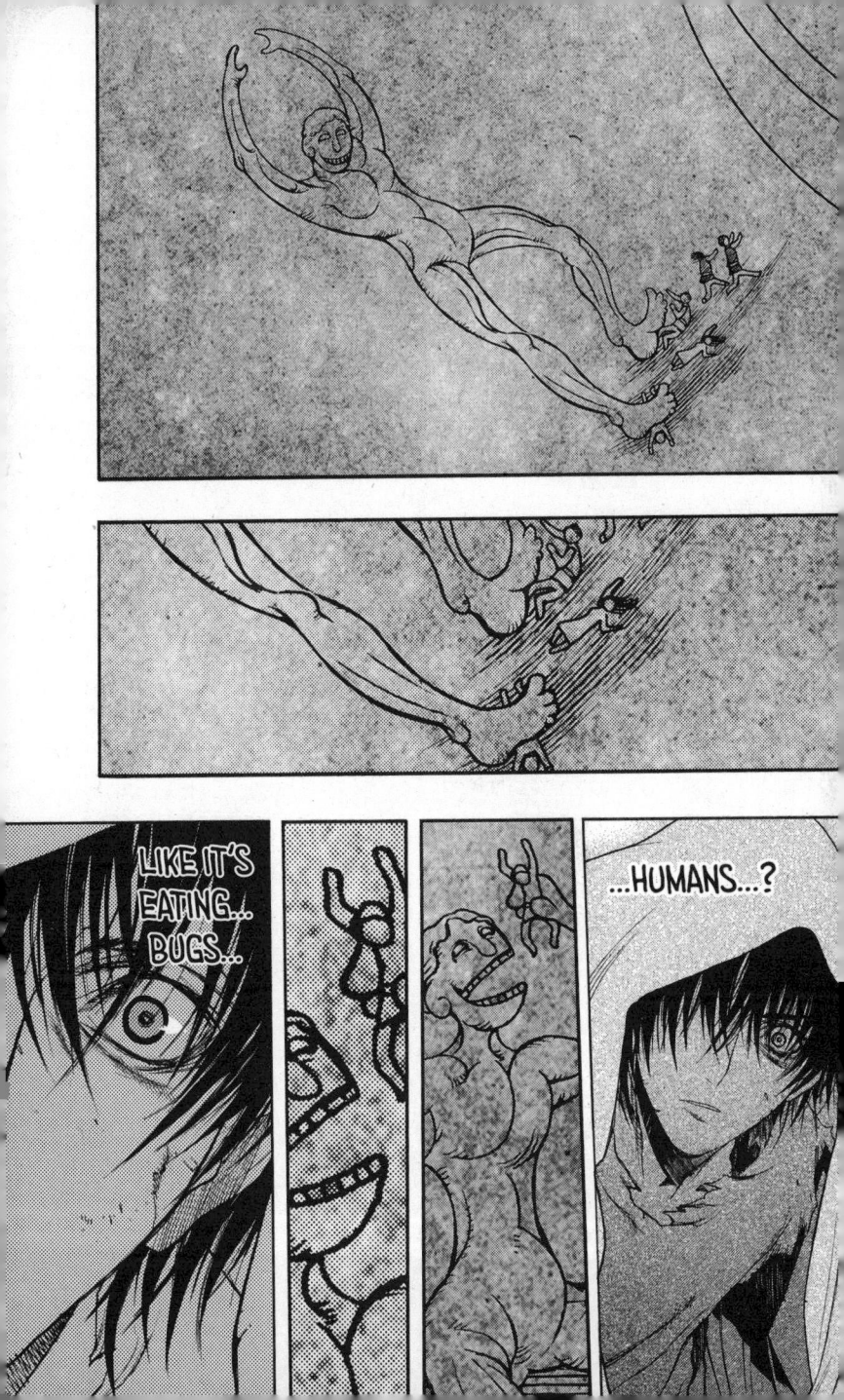
LIKE IT'S EATING... BUGS...
...HUMANS...?

RATTLE
SO THIS IS... WHY THEY AFRAID...
...OF ME...
I WISH I COULD DO SOME-THING FOR YOU...
I WANT TO SEE...
WHAT... IS TITAN?

...IF I AM... NOT SON OF TITAN...
AND... FIND OUT...
SHARLE...
TO DO IT...
TELL ME...
...ABOUT THE HUMAN WORLD...

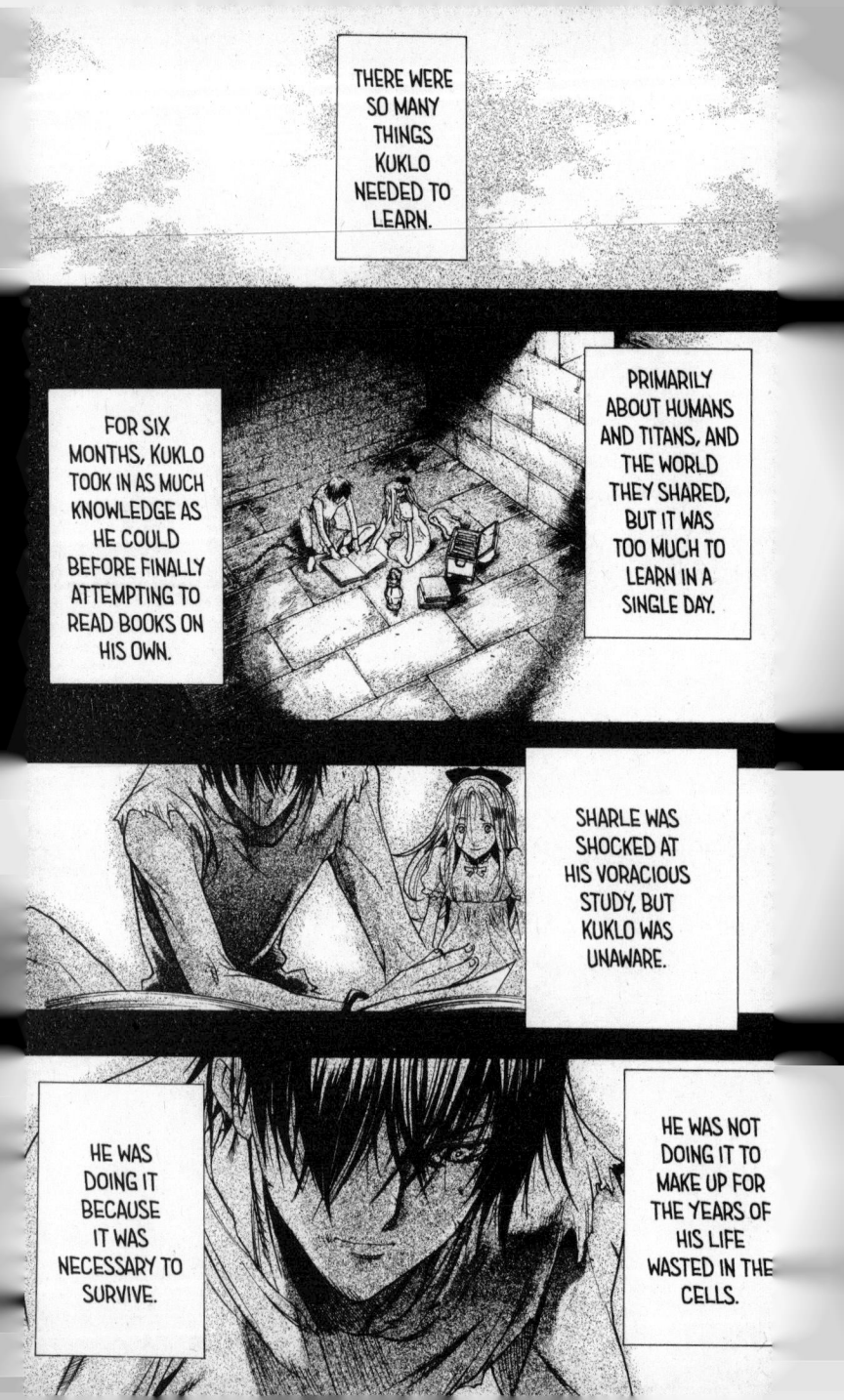
THERE WERE SO MANY THINGS KUKLO NEEDED TO LEARN.
FOR SIX MONTHS, KUKLO TOOK IN AS MUCH KNOWLEDGE AS HE COULD BEFORE FINALLY ATTEMPTING TO READ BOOKS ON HIS OWN.
PRIMARILY ABOUT HUMANS AND TITANS, AND THE WORLD THEY SHARED, BUT IT WAS TOO MUCH TO LEARN IN A SINGLE DAY.
SHARLE WAS SHOCKED AT HIS VORACIOUS STUDY, BUT KUKLO WAS UNAWARE.
HE WAS DOING IT BECAUSE IT WAS NECESSARY TO SURVIVE.
HE WAS NOT DOING IT TO MAKE UP FOR THE YEARS OF HIS LIFE WASTED IN THE CELLS.

KUKLO DID NOT DEDICATE HIMSELF TO STUDY ALONE.
AT THE SAME TIME, HE WAS PLOTTING AN ESCAPE FROM THE CELLAR.
AFTER ALL, HE COULDN'T PUT HIS NEWFOUND KNOWLEDGE TO USE, TRAPPED IN A CELL.
JUST CUT THE CHAINS.
OF COURSE, A HEAVY FRETSAW WOULD ONLY ATTRACT ATTENTION.
HE CHOSE A MUCH LONGER AND PATIENT METHOD: TO ROT AWAY HIS CHAINS WITHOUT DETECTION THROUGH SWEAT, BLOOD AND URINE.

HE KNEW THEY WOULD NEVER RELEASE HIM.
HE HAD NO INTENTION OF SPEAKING WITH XAVI AND DARIO.
THIS WOULD SUPPOSEDLY GIVE XAVI COURAGE AND CONFIDENCE AS HE STROVE TO LEAD THE MILITARY.
DARIO BOUGHT KUKLO SO THAT XAVI COULD PUNISH THE "TITAN'S SON."
"I'VE VAN-QUISHED ONE OF THOSE TITANS."
NO DOUBT XAVI WOULD PUFF OUT HIS CHEST AND BOAST...
AS LONG AS HIS CONCEITS WERE FULFILLED, IT ENDED QUICKLY.
AS PAINFUL AS IT WAS, XAVI'S RELIANCE ON VIOLENCE MADE HIM ALMOST PITIFULLY EASY TO CONTROL.

SO KUKLO PLAYED THE PART OF THE TITAN'S SON...
IN THE END...
ALL TO KEEP XAVI AND DARIO UNAWARE OF HIS PLAN.
...IT TOOK TWO YEARS BEFORE ALL OF HIS PREPARATIONS WERE COMPLETE.
HA
HA
HA!

SO YOU'RE ABOUT TO ENTER TRAINING, XAVI.
ARE YOU READY FOR IT?
ONE DAY, I'LL BE RUNNING THE MILITARY.
I'VE BEEN READY MY ENTIRE LIFE, FATHER.
S IT JUST HE INTIMACY OF FAMILY?

TWO YEARS OF SUBJUGATING KUKLO HAS INSTILLED TRUE CONFIDENCE IN MY BROTHER.
THE SKILL TO BECOME A STRONG LEADER...
BY THE WAY, FATHER...
...OR PERHAPS THAT'S JUST WHAT HE THINKS...
WHAT W HAPPE AFTER I LEFT?
HAPPEN TO WHAT?
TO IT.
AHH...
IT.
"IT," THEY CALL HIM....

MAYBE THEY'LL JUST LET HIM GO FREE...
I'M GOING TO THE BARRACKS, SO WE DON'T NEED IT ANYMORE, DO WE?
WHEN THEY REALLY MEAN **KUKLO...**
INDEED. THERE'S NO POINT TO KEEPING IT **HERE.**
...OF COURSE...
LET'S SELL IT OFF, THEN!
I'M SURE THE BUYERS WILL BE LINING UP!
AND I'LL HAVE TO SAY GOODBYE TO HIM VERY SOON...
BUT THAT MEANS... EVERYTHING MUST HAPPEN ON A FASTER SCHEDULE.
SHARLE.
HIS LIFE IS FINALLY BEGINNING. I MUST SEE HIM OFF WITH A SMILE...
NOTHING GOOD WILL COME FROM KUKLO BEING HERE...

I KNOW IT'S HARD TO SAY GOODBYE TO XAVI, BUT IT'S NOT LIKE YOU'LL NEVER SEE HIM AGAIN.
HAVE... HAVE I?
HUH?
WHAT'S TH MATTER? YOU'VE GO QUIET.
THAT'S RIGHT.
MUNCH
MUNCH
I AM...?
YOU'RE ABOUT TO BE VERY BUSY.
AND THERE'S LITTLE TIME FOR MOURNING.
!
THE ARRANGEMENT FOR YOUR MARRIAGE WILL BE FINALIZED VERY SOON.
NOW IT'S MY TURN TO BE TRAPPED IN A CELL...
I'M ONLY A TOOL OF MY FATHER'S, AS WELL...
THAT'S RIGHT...
MARR IAGE..

TWO YEARS...
..PASSED
.O FAST...
WHEN I GET OUT...I MUST TAKE THIS OFF...

FOR THE REST...
...I JUST HAVE TO BE DETERMINED...
KNOCK KNOCK
コン! コン!
CRE
AAAK
...I WOULD STILL BE THE TITAN'S SON...
IF NOT FOR SHARLE...

I WANT...
...TO LEAVE... THIS PLACE...

SHARLE...
SHE'S... CRYING?

FATHER SAYS...
...HE'S GOING TO SELL YOU OFF...

THEY DON'T...
...NEED ME... ANY-MORE...
...IS LEAVING HOME...
MY BROTH-ER...
ME?
YES... SO I'LL BRING YOU SOME THINGS TOMORROW NIGHT.
...I MUST... HURRY TO ESCAPE ...?
THEN ...
THERE'S NOT MUCH TIME... I THINK THEY'LL FIND YOU A NEW OWNER WITHIN A FEW DAYS...
...THANK YOU.
IT'S ENOUGH.
JUST SOME CLOTHES... AND MONEY...
I'M GOING, TOO...
ZZT...

I'LL HAVE TO LEAVE HOME SOON...
I'M GOING TO BE MARRIED AWAY...
...
OH...

SHARLE...
WHAT DO YOU WANT TO DO ...?
SAY NO, IF YOU DON'T LIKE IT.
IF IT WAS...
... REALLY THAT EASY ...
YOU CAN.
I CAN'T!
I DON'T HAVE ANY OTHER CHOICE!
THEN...

COME WITH ME?

HUH...?

I WILL TAKE BACK... MY LIFE.
THAT'S WHY I LEAVE.

IT'S BAD TO BE IN A CAGE.
YOU LEAVE TOO, SHARLE.

BUT... I...
...I'M NOT... STRONG LIKE YOU...

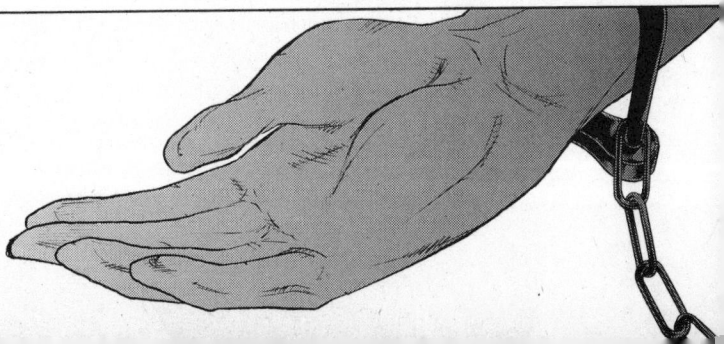

LET'S GO TOGETHER.

LEAVE EVERY-THING TO ME.

Chapter 3: Moonlit Oath END

ATTACK ON TITAN
BEFORE THE FALL

TO BE CONTINUED

The following 12-page story, "Attack on Titan: Before the Fall: Trailer," is something like a pilot version of this story that was originally run in the magazine as a prologue. Because of this, some events may differ from the finished story.

THE FALL OF WALL MARIA.

THE FATEFUL DAY

...ON WHICH HUMANITY LOST...

...A THIRD OF ITS SAFE HARBOR...

BUT FEW KNEW OF THE FACT THAT **THEY** ONCE BREACHED OUR WALLS 70 YEARS AGO...

...FOR DESPITE THE MANY VICTIMS OF THAT DISASTER, THE ROYAL GOVERNMENT FORBADE THE PEOPLE TO SPEAK OF IT, AND ERASED ALL TRACES OF IT FROM RECORD...

BUT IT REALLY DID HAPPEN

...THE FADING MEMORY...
...THAT DAY BROUGHT BACK...
AFTER 30 YEARS OF PEACE...

ATTACK ON TITAN
BEFORE THE FALL
Trailer
...INTO THEIR HEARTS!!!
...AND CARVED IT DEEP...
...OF HUMANITY'S TERRIBLE FOE...

ZMF...
ZMF...
IL...
WHA ...?
A... TITAN ...?
ZMF...
ZMF...
BUT HOW ...?!

WALL MARIA IS STILL STANDING!

ズ!
ZMFF
ZMF
ZMF
ズ!
ZMF
ズ!
ZMF
ズ!
ZMF
ゴゴゴ

AH...
AH...
AH...
AH...
GRSHK
AAAAAAH!!
RAAHH!

GREAT, GLORIOUS TITAN...
OHHH...

KSHUNK
AT THIS TIME...

*This "Trailer" was originally run in the October 2013 issue of Monthly Shonen Sirius as a prologue.

ATTACK ON TITAN

BEFORE THE FALL

WANT MORE TITAN?
The following pages contain a preview of "Attack on Titan: Junior High," a parody spin-off of "Attack on Titan" that recasts your favorite characters as junior high students!
Vol. 1 includes over 300 pages of Titanic comedy!
ATTACK on TITAN
JUNIOR HIGH
Vol. 1 available now from Kodansha Comics!

... HON-ESTLY!
I'M GETTING WORRIED THAT WE MIGHT NEVER GET BACK!
RUSTLE
THIS FOREST GOES A LOT FARTHER THAN I THOUGHT...
RUSTLE
RUSTLE
RUSTLE
AWW
IT'S COMING CLOSER.
THUD
THUD
THUD
THUD
... DID YOU HEAR SOME-THING?
THUD
IT'S ALL BECAUSE YOU DECIDED WE'D STRIKE OUT ON OUR OWN ON THIS FIELD TRIP, EREN...
THUD
THUD
THUD
A-AWW, SHUT UP!!
WAAAAHHH!

FIVE YEARS LATER..
WE'RE FINALLY JUNIOR HIGH SCHOOL STUDENTS, HUH?
IT'S SUPER EXCITING, RIGHT, MIKASA?!
YOU KNOW WHAT ENTERING JUNIOR HIGH MEANS...!
WHY DO YOU LOOK SO GLUM?!
.....
CAN'T SAY I FEEL THAT WAY.

HUSSSSH
IT'S OUR CHANCE TO DEFEAT THE...
TI-TAKGH !!
BONNK
IT'S ONE THEIR ERASERS, RIGHT?
I THINK SO, BUT...
UGH... THIS ERASER'S BIGGER THAN MY RAGE ISSUES!
GWHP
ZLIK
ZLIK
ERE
STOP THAT !!
ZLIK
ZLIK
I'LL GOUGE MY NAME INTO IT! THAT'LL SHOW 'EM!!
WOOD CARVING KIT
ZWIP

OKAY ...
THE PENGUIN SAYS I SHOULD LISTEN TO YOU.
REMEMBER WHAT THE DOCTOR SAID. TAKE A DEEP BREATH, COUNT TO TEN, AND CONTACT YOUR POWER ANIMAL.
...BUT SOMEONE PROBABLY JUST DROPPED IT.
YES, IT'S ONE OF THEIR ERASERS...
ERE
STABB
...WOR RRGK !!
JUST WAIT... I'LL PAY YOU BASTARDS BACK TENFOLD FOR WHAT YOU MADE ME SUFFER... MARK MY—
BUT B CAREF IN JR HIGH WE'LL AT WA WITH TH EVER DAY.
Eh?
D-DAMN IT ...
THIS IS THE LAST STRAW...
KATONK
OWWWWW!!
RUSTLE
RUSTLE
I WILL NEVER FORGIVE YOU !!
RUMMBLE

DOOOOOM
YOU WON'T GET AWAY WITH THIS, TITAN!!
HEY!
スッ
FWIP

GLPTF
VWOOSH
...
EREN
MURMUR
MURMUR
MURMUR
You are such a tool, Eren.
C'mon, fight like a man!
GRUNCH
BUT WE CALL IT WALL MARIA.
THIS IS THE GATE OF ATTACK JUNIOR HIGH SCHOOL.

WHEN ARE YOU GOING TO SHUT UP ABOUT THE TITANS?
WHAT ARE YOU SAYING, MIKASA?
JUST YOU WAIT AND SEE! I'M GONNA TAKE DOWN HIM AND ALL HIS FRIENDS! I'M GONNA BEAT ALL THE TITANS!
IT'S HIS OWN FAULT FOR DROPPING IT, ANYWAY!
FIGHTING TITANS IS DANGEROUSLY IDIOTIC, EVEN FOR YOU..
CHATTER
...I WANT YOU TO STOP OBSESSING OVER THEM.
I KNOW THAT INCIDENT FROM FIVE YEARS AGO MADE YOU HATE THEM, BUT...
Security Checkpoint Human Entrance
CHATTER
YOU DON'T WANT THAT SECRET ABOUT FIVE YEARS AGO TO GET OUT...
MORE THAN ANYTHING ELSE...
AND...

THEY DON'T HAVE A CLUE THAT I'VE INFILTRATED THEIR RANKS!
HEH! STUPID TITANS!
Security Checkpoint Titan Entrance
EREN?
ペロン SLUMP
MY TICKET TO VEN-GEANCE!
WHAT IS IT...
THEN THE TEACHER WILL SCOLD THEM FOR FORGETTING IT, AND I WILL GIGGLE IN TRIUMPH!
I KNOW I'LL STEA SOMETHI FROM ON OF THEM
オウ BLEAAARRRGGHH
SOME KIND O CLOTH
GRIMP

RUSTLE
SHUFFLE
BWAAAHHN
もわぁぁぁん
MPH! IT STINKS WORSE THAN DAD'S MUSTACHE!!
DAMN IT! IT FELL ON TOP OF ME...!
RUSTLE
FWOOSH
TUGG
EUGH!! IT SMELLS AWFUL!
WHATEVER! I'LL JUST GET THE STUPID THING WITH ONE BIG PULL!
?!
UT WHAT
S IT...?
TWIRL
I MUST'VE NICKED SOMETHING BIG!
GAG! SWEET FREEDOM...
GYM SHORTS

MIKASA !!
ズーリ ZLIMM ズーリ ZLIMM
It stinks anyway.
BURN IT WITH FIRE.
WHAT ARE YOU DOING, EREN?!
ギュ
THEY'RE GYM SHORTS, AND THEY'RE NOT WHAT I MEANT TO STEAL! THAT IS...
SO YOU'RE THE PANTY THIEF?!
HEY!! WHAT ARE TWO HUMAN STUDENTS DOING HERE?
YOU RATTED ME OUT ...?!
...REFUSE TO BOW MY HEAD TO ANY TITAN...
THIRL
I MEAN, WHAT KIND OF TITAN...
WHAT?! NO WAY! I...
THE STUDEN WHOSE PANT-IES YO STOLE I IN TEAR APOLO-GIZE, PERVO

HIK
SNIFF
JUST LOOK AT HOW SAD SHE IS!!
SNIFF
SNIFF
AND THEN, I...
...DID THAT...
...TO THAT...
THAT...
SNIFF
.....
You'll never become a full-fledged adult like that...!
...
STOMP
STOMP
!!
SERIOUSLY? YOU FAINTED?
YOU'RE WORSE AT APOLOGIZING THAN SHIA LEBOEUF.
SLUMP
EREN ?!

CHATTER
CHATTER
1st Year, Class
...ON THE OTHER HAND, EREN 100%, COMPLETELY, WITHOUT A DOUBT, SURE AS A TITAN VOMITS IN THE WOODS, BROUGHT THIS ON HIMSELF...
NOW THAT I KNOW WHAT HAPPENED, THERE'S A CHANCE HE WANTS ME TO COMFORT HIM...
WHIMPER
WHIRL
...
...
EREN!
YOU FEEL BETTER ALREADY ...?
MIKASA ...
SKRRT
...THAT MIGHT JUST HURT HIS PRIDE...
SO IF I WERE TO COMFORT HIM...
...EREN PROBABL KNOWS TH TOO...

...HUH?
HOW ABOUT A HUG?
DON'T YOU THINK YOU'RE ACTING A LITTLE COLD, MIKASA?
...
...
I FIGURED THAT IF I WERE YOU, I'D COMFORT ME, SO I WAITED QUIETLY...
BECAUSE HE WAS A TITAN, SO HE HAS TO BE EVIL, EVEN IF I CAN'T TELL HOW.
NO, I DIDN'T DO ANYTHING WRONG.
...NO, UM... EREN...
I THOUGHT YOU BROUGHT THAT ON YOURSELF, SO...
HUH?

**Read more in Attack on Titan: Junior High Vol. 1, available now!**

Chihiro has an unusual connection to zombie movies. He doesn't feel bad for the survivors – he wants to comfort the undead girls they slaughter! When his pet passes away, he brews a resurrection potion. He's discovered by local heiress Sanka Rea, and she serves as his first test subject!

KODANSHA COMICS

NO.6
A PERFECT LIFE IN A PERFECT CITY
For Shion, an elite student in the technologically sophisticated city No. 6, life is carefully choreographed. One fateful day, he takes a misstep, sheltering a fugitive his age from a typhoon. Helping this boy throws Shion's life down a path to discovering the appalling secrets behind the "perfection" of No. 6.
KODAN COMI
© Atsuko Asano and Hinoki Kino/Kodansha Ltd. All rights reserved.

Rec
Reading
Fiction
S

*Attack on Titan: Before the Fall* volume 1 is a work of fiction. Names, characters, places, and incidents are the products of the author's imagination or are used fictitiously. Any resemblance to actual events, locales, or persons, living or dead, is entirely coincidental.

A Kodansha Comics Trade Paperback Original
*Attack on Titan: Before the Fall* volume 1 copyright © 2013 Hajime Isayama/Ryo Suzukaze/Satoshi Shiki
English translation copyright © 2014 Hajime Isayama/Ryo Suzukaze/Satoshi Shiki

All rights reserved.

Published in the United States by Kodansha Comics, an imprint of Kodansha USA Publishing, LLC, New York.

Publication rights for this English edition arranged through Kodansha Ltd, Tokyo.

First published in Japan in 2013 by Kodansha Ltd., Tokyo as *Shingeki no kyojin Before the fall*, volume 1.

ISBN 978-1-61262-910-0

Character designs by Thores Shibamoto
Original cover design by Takashi Shimoyama (Red Rooster)

Printed in the United States of America.

www.kodanshacomics.com

9 8 7 6 5 4 3 2
Translation: Stephen Paul
Lettering: Steve Wands
Editing: Ben Applegate